W9-AVK-588

This edition published by Parragon Books Ltd in 2016 and distributed by

Parragon Inc.
440 Park Avenue South, 13th Floor
New York, NY 10016
www.parragon.com

Written and retold by Etta Saunders, Catherine Allison, Peter Bently, Claire Sipi,
Anne Rooney, Ronne Randall, Anne Marie Ryan
Illustrated by Deborah Allwright, Victoria Assanelli, Deborah Melmon, Jacqueline East,
Erica-Jane Waters, Livia Coloji, Sean Julian, Maria Bogade, Dubravka Kolanovic,
Tamsin and Natalie Hinrichsen
Edited by Rebecca Wilson
Cover illustrated by Charlotte Cooke

Every effort has been made to acknowledge the contributors to this book.
If we have made any errors, we will be pleased to rectify them in future editions.

ISBN 978-1-4723-5467-9

Printed in China

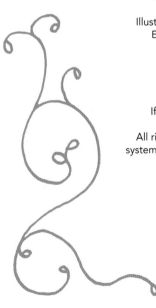

A Collection of
Stories for
5
Year Olds

PaRragon

Bath · New York · Cologne · Melbourne · Delhi
Hong Kong · Shenzhen · Singapore

Contents

Pinocchio

There was once a carpenter named
Geppetto. One day, he found a magic
piece of talking wood in an enchanted
forest. "How unusual!" he thought.

Geppetto took the magic wood home and
carved a little puppet boy from it. He gave
the boy some clothes and a hat. The wooden
boy danced around the room for Geppetto
and made him laugh.

"Hello!" he said.

Geppetto named the boy Pinocchio. "You must go to school like the other children," Geppetto told him.

On the way to school Pinocchio met a cricket.

"I will help you to learn right from wrong," the cricket told Pinocchio.

Then Pinocchio met a fox and a cat. They had heard the sound of lunch money in his pocket.

"Don't go to school," said the fox. "Play with us instead!" Pinocchio thought that sounded like a good idea.

"I don't think you are doing the right thing," the cricket told him.

But Pinocchio didn't listen to the cricket.

The cat and the fox led Pinocchio into a dark forest.

"If you plant money here, it will grow into a money tree," they said.

"I don't think you are doing the right thing," the cricket told him.

But Pinocchio didn't listen to the cricket. He dug a hole in the ground and buried the coins in it.

Then Pinocchio went home. He did not tell his father that he hadn't been to school.

Pinocchio didn't go to school the next day, either. He wanted to find his money tree instead.

So the cricket followed Pinocchio into the forest. But the money tree wasn't there!

Pinocchio dug the ground to look for his coins ... They were all gone!

"The fox and the cat tricked you to get your money," said the cricket.

Pinocchio felt silly. He pretended he didn't care and stomped off into the forest.

"I'm going on an adventure," he said.

The little cricket begged Pinocchio to go home, but the wooden boy walked on.

Darkness fell and Pinocchio soon felt scared.

They came to a tiny cottage, and Pinocchio knocked loudly on the door.

A pretty fairy with turquoise hair answered.

"We're lost," explained Pinocchio. "Please can you help us?"

The fairy invited them inside and gave them some food.

"Why are you so far from home?" she asked kindly.

Pinocchio did not want to tell her that he had disobeyed his father.

"I was chased by a giant!" he lied.

Suddenly, Pinocchio's nose grew.

"The giant was taller than the trees …" he continued.

Pinocchio's nose grew some more.

"I ran into the forest to escape!" he added. Pinocchio's nose grew again, and he touched it in wonder.

"I have put a spell on you!" said the fairy. "Every time you tell a lie, your wooden nose will grow."

Pinocchio began to cry. He wished he had gone to school like his father had said!

"I won't tell any more lies," he promised.

The fairy called some friendly woodpeckers. They pecked at Pinocchio's long nose until it was back to normal.

In the morning, Pinocchio rushed home with the little cricket perched on his shoulder.

"From now on, I will do as Father tells me," he said.

But Geppetto wasn't home. There, on the kitchen table, Pinocchio found a note.

Dear Pinocchio,
I have gone to look for you. I miss you, my son.
Your loving father, Geppetto.

Pinocchio was sad. He had caused a lot of trouble. So he set off with the cricket to find his father and bring him home.

They began their search by the river. Pinocchio stood too near the edge of the water, and he fell in with a splash! The cricket jumped in to help, but they were both swallowed by an enormous fish.

Luckily, they found Geppetto in the fish's tummy!

Pinocchio hugged his father tightly. "I won't leave you again!" he said.

Then the clever wooden boy had an idea. He took the feather from his hat and tickled the fish.

"A … a … a … choo!" The fish sneezed, and Geppetto, Pinocchio, and the cricket shot out of the fish's mouth. They landed safely on the bank of the river.

That night, Pinocchio was sleeping in his own bed when the fairy with turquoise hair flew in through his window.

"You are a good, brave boy," she said, kissing him on the forehead.

In the morning, Pinocchio found that he was no longer made from wood. He was a real boy! From then on, he was always a good son to Geppetto. And his friend the cricket didn't need to tell him right from wrong, ever again.

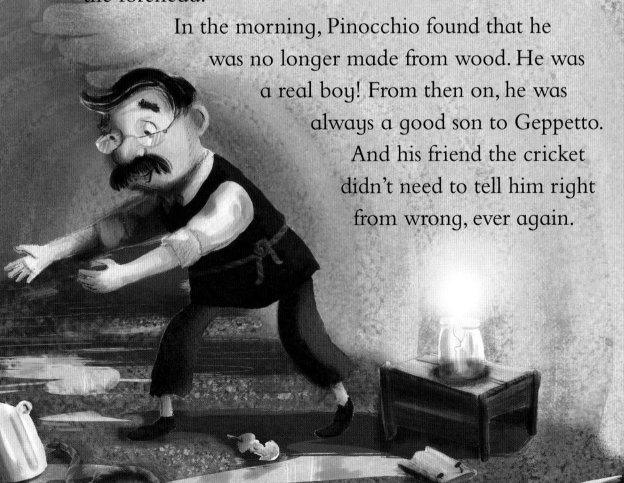

How the Leopard Got His Spots

Long ago, Leopard lived on a sandy-yellow plain in Africa. Giraffe and Zebra and some deer lived there, too. The animals were sandy yellow all over, just like the plain itself.

Leopard was also sandy yellow. This wasn't good for the rest of the animals because Leopard could hide in the sandy yellow grasses. Then he would jump out and eat them up!

Giraffe and Zebra and the rest of the animals lived in fear. But Leopard was very happy and never hungry!

Soon the animals were fed up with running away from Leopard. So they moved to a huge forest where the sun shone through the trees. It made stripy and spotted and patchy shadows on the ground.

The animals hid themselves there, partly in the sun, partly in the shadows.

Soon their skins changed color. Giraffe became covered with brown patches from the patchy shadow he stood in. Zebra became stripy from the stripy shadow he lay in. The other animals became darker, too, with spotted patterns and wavy lines from the shadows around them.

Back on the sandy plain, Leopard was feeling hungry.

"Where has everyone gone?" he asked Baboon.

"To the forest," said Baboon carelessly. "And they've changed. You need to change, too."

Leopard wasn't sure what Baboon meant, but he set out for the forest anyway.

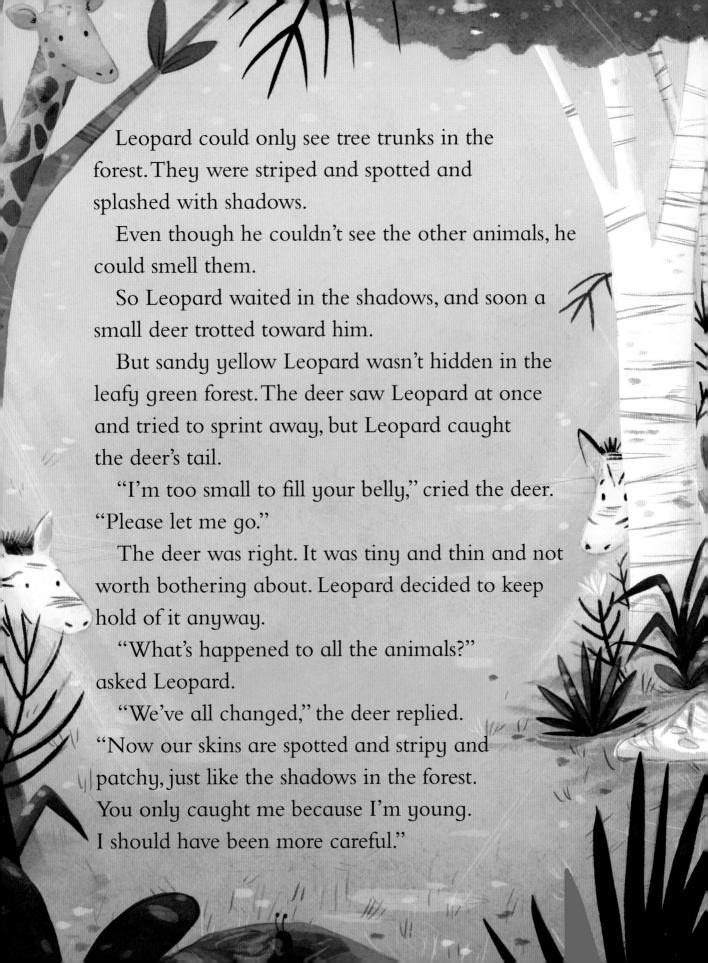

Leopard could only see tree trunks in the forest. They were striped and spotted and splashed with shadows.

Even though he couldn't see the other animals, he could smell them.

So Leopard waited in the shadows, and soon a small deer trotted toward him.

But sandy yellow Leopard wasn't hidden in the leafy green forest. The deer saw Leopard at once and tried to sprint away, but Leopard caught the deer's tail.

"I'm too small to fill your belly," cried the deer. "Please let me go."

The deer was right. It was tiny and thin and not worth bothering about. Leopard decided to keep hold of it anyway.

"What's happened to all the animals?" asked Leopard.

"We've all changed," the deer replied. "Now our skins are spotted and stripy and patchy, just like the shadows in the forest. You only caught me because I'm young. I should have been more careful."

Leopard let the little deer go and sat down to think.
"So that's why I can't see the animals in the forest,"
he thought. "They've changed their skins to match the
shadowy trees. If I'm going to catch them, do I need to
change, too? And how in the world can I do that?"

More deer walked through the trees. Leopard could see them clearly when they moved, but the shadows hid them when they stopped.

Leopard was easy to spot with his sandy yellow skin, so the deer stayed away.

Leopard sat in the shadows a long time and licked his paws thoughtfully. Soon he noticed his paws had dark spots on them. And there were spots on his tail, too!

Leopard looked around and realized that the spots on his skin matched the small patches of shadow he was lying in.

"Ah-ha!" he thought. "The shadows have made these spots. That's how I can change my skin like the other animals!"

Leopard had grown tired from all the thinking and waiting. So he lay down and fell into a deep sleep.

When he awoke, his skin was covered in dark spots made by the shadows of the forest.

"How wonderful!" he said, looking at his new skin. "Now I can hide in the forest like the other animals. When they come close, I'll catch them and eat them up!"

Leopard lived happily in the forest, eating and sleeping and NOT being spotted.

And the other animals learned to hide from him as well as they could, too!

Bunny Loves to Read

Buster Bunny loved books.

One day, his friends came over to see him.

"Hi Buster!" they said. "Are you coming out to play?"

"Sure," said Buster with a smile, "when I've finished my book. It's all about pirates!"

"You've always got your nose in a book!" said his sister Bella. "Hopscotch is much more fun!"

"Books are boring!" croaked Francine.

"Why read books when you can play leapfrog?"

"Reading is not as much fun as racing each other," agreed Max.

"Don't listen to them, Buster," said Sam.
"I think books are the best!"
    "Really?" asked Buster.

    "Yes," said Sam, smiling. "Books are the best—for nibbling!"
"Oh no, you don't," laughed Buster.

Then Bella said, "Come on, let's leave Buster with his dumb old books and play outside!"

But it was raining. The friends looked out of the window gloomily.

"Why don't you read some of my books?" asked Buster, bringing out a big box.

"OK," said Sam grumpily. "Just while we wait for the rain to stop."

Awhile later, Buster looked
out of the window.
"Hey, it's stopped raining!"
he cried. "Who's coming out
to play?"

Shh! I'm reading.
The pirates are
looking for treasure!

26

When the friends had finally finished reading, they went outside.

"So what do you want to play?" asked Buster.

"Let's pretend we can do magic spells. If you give me a kiss, I'll turn into a princess!" said Francine.

"Ugh! No thanks!" laughed Sam. "Let's play pirates!"

28

"Look out," said Bella.
"I'm a Tyrannosaurus!"

ROOAAR

"I'm off to find the
enchanted princess!"
cried Max.

They played pirates and dinosaurs and princes and princesses until it was time to go home.

"Do you have any other books about dinosaurs?" asked Bella.

"Sure!" said Buster.

"What about frogs?" asked Francine.

"Yes," said Buster. "And toads, too."

"Anything else about witches and magic?" asked Max.

"Loads!"

"Can I borrow another pirate story?" Sam asked.

"Of course, you can," laughed Buster, "as long as you promise not to eat it!"

Snow White

Once there was a queen who wanted a daughter.

As she sat sewing by her window one winter's day, she pricked her finger on the needle. Three drops of blood fell from her finger.

"I wish I could have a daughter with blood-red lips, ebony-black hair, and skin as white as snow," she thought.

Soon the queen gave birth to a baby girl. She had blood-red lips, ebony hair, and skin as white as snow. The Queen named her Snow White.

Sadly, the queen died and the king married again.

His new bride was beautiful but vain.

The queen had a magic mirror, and every day she asked it:

"Mirror, mirror, on the wall,
Who is the fairest of them all?"
And the mirror would reply:

"You, O Queen, are the fairest
of them all."

Meanwhile, Snow White
grew into a beautiful girl.
One morning, the queen
asked the mirror who was the
fairest. The mirror replied:

"You, O Queen, are fair, it's true,
But young Snow White
is fairer than you."

The queen was furious. "Take Snow White into the
forest and kill her!" she told her huntsman.
The huntsman led Snow White deep into the
forest, but he did not want to hurt her.
"Run away as far from here as you can," he said.
So Snow White fled into the forest.

It was getting dark when Snow White came upon a little cottage. She knocked on the door, but there was no answer.

Snow White was so tired that she went inside anyway. She found a table and seven tiny chairs and seven little beds.

Snow White lay down on the seventh bed and fell asleep.

She awoke to find seven little men staring at her in amazement.

"Who are you?" she asked.

"We are the seven dwarves who live here," said one dwarf. "Who are you?"

"I am Snow White," she replied. She told them her sad story.

"You can stay here with us," the eldest dwarf said kindly.

Every day, the seven dwarves went off to work in the mines while Snow White stayed behind to cook and clean for them.

"Do not open the door to anyone," the dwarves told Snow White. They were worried the wicked queen would find her.

That day, the wicked queen asked her mirror who was the fairest. The mirror replied:

"You, O Queen, are fair, it's true,
But Snow White is still fairer than you.
Deep in the forest with seven little men,
Snow White is living in a cozy den."

The wicked queen was furious and vowed that she would kill Snow White herself! So she added poison to a juicy apple and disguised herself as a pedlar woman. Then she set off into the forest.

She knocked at the door of the dwarves' cottage.

"Try my fresh apples," the disguised queen called out.

Snow White remembered the dwarves' warning and opened the window instead of the door.

The queen offered Snow White an apple. The girl hesitated before taking a big bite. But the poisoned piece got stuck in her throat, and she fell to the ground.

The seven dwarves were heartbroken to find their beloved Snow White dead. They made a glass coffin for her and placed it in the forest. Then they took turns watching over it.

One day, a prince rode by.

"Who is this beautiful girl?" asked the prince.

The dwarves told him the sad story.

"Please let me take her away," begged the prince. "I promise I will watch over her."

The dwarves could see the prince loved Snow White and agreed to let her go.

But the prince's servants lost their grip on the coffin, and it slipped. The fall jolted the piece of poisoned apple from Snow White's throat, and she came back to life.

Snow White fell in love with the kind
and handsome prince, and the couple were
soon married.

The dwarves joined them in the prince's
large castle, and they all lived happily
together forever.

Rumpelstiltskin

Once upon a time, a poor miller had a beautiful daughter.

One day, the king rode through the village. The miller wanted to impress the king, so he told him a lie.

"Your Highness, my daughter can spin straw into gold!" he fibbed.

"This I must see," replied the king.

So the next day, the miller took his daughter to the palace. The king led the girl to a room filled with straw. On the floor stood a little stool and a spinning wheel.

"Spin this straw into gold by tomorrow morning, or you will be thrown into the dungeon," said the king. Then he left the room and locked the door.

The miller's daughter wept at the impossible task before her.

All of a sudden, the door sprang open and in leapt the strangest little man she had ever seen.

"Why are you crying?" he asked.

"I have to spin all this straw into gold before the morning," replied the girl sadly, "but I don't know how."

"If you give me your pretty necklace, I will spin the straw into gold," said the strange little man.

"Oh, thank you!" cried the girl, handing him her necklace.

The little man sat down in front of the spinning wheel and set to work.

The little man spun all night long. By morning, the room was filled with reels of gold. And just as suddenly as he had appeared, the strange little man disappeared.

The next day, the king was astonished to see so much gold.

"You have done very well," he told the miller's daughter, "but I wonder if you can do the same thing again?"

So he took the girl to a much bigger room. It, too, was filled with straw.

"Spin this into gold by tomorrow morning, or you will be thrown into the dungeon," said the king. Then he locked the door as before.

The miller's daughter was very frightened. But the strange little man appeared again.

"Don't cry," he said. "Give me your shiny ring, and I will spin the straw into gold."

So she did, and the little man set to work. Again, by morning, all the straw was turned into gold.

"If you can do this once more, you shall be my queen!" cried the king.

The poor miller's daughter wept even more this time when the king left.

"Why are you crying?" asked the little man, appearing for the third time. "You know that I will help you."

"But I have nothing left to give you," sobbed the girl.

"If you become queen," replied the little man, "you can give me your firstborn child."

The miller's daughter agreed. And once again, all the straw was spun into gold.

The next day, the king was delighted to see all the gold. So he kept his promise and married the miller's daughter.

The new queen was very happy and soon forgot all about the strange little man.

But when she had a baby boy, the man appeared again.

The queen was horrified. "Please don't take my son!" she begged. "Take all my jewels and money instead."

"No! You made a promise," replied the strange little man. "But I will give you three days. If you can guess my name, you will keep your baby."

The queen agreed. The next day, she sent her messengers out to collect as many boys' names as possible from all over the kingdom.

That night, the queen read out the names to the strange little man. But he just laughed.

So the next day, the messengers went out to find even more names. But once again, the queen's guesses were wrong.

On the third day, the poor queen was in despair. It was getting late by the time her last messenger returned.

"Your Highness, I haven't found any new names," he said, "but I saw a little man in the forest leaping and dancing around a fire. He sang this song:

"*The queen will never win my game,*

For Rumpelstiltskin is my name!"

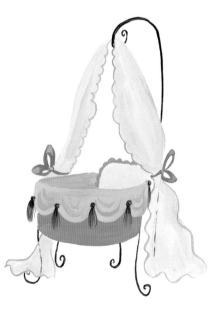

The queen was overjoyed!

When the little man appeared that night, she asked him, "Are you perhaps named … Rumpelstiltskin?"

The little man was furious, and he stamped his foot so hard it went through the floor. Then he stomped out of the room and was never seen again.

And the king and queen and their son lived happily ever after.

Aladdin

Once upon a time, a boy named Aladdin lived with his mother. They were very poor and often hungry.

One day, a man visited their shack. He said he was Aladdin's long-lost uncle and wanted to help Aladdin make his fortune. Aladdin and his mother were delighted.

So Aladdin traveled with the man into the desert until they came to a rock. The man pushed the rock aside to reveal a hidden cave.

"Climb down into this cave and fetch a lamp that you will find there," the man told Aladdin. "Bring it to me. Don't touch anything except the lamp. Wear this magic ring to protect you."

Aladdin dared not argue with his uncle. He put on the magic ring and climbed into the cave. As soon as he was through the entrance, his eyes grew wide with wonder. Piles of gold and jewels stretched from floor to ceiling. But Aladdin did as he had promised and touched nothing. At last, he found a dull brass lamp.

"Surely this can't be it?" Aladdin thought, but he took it back to his uncle. Aladdin soon found that he was unable to climb out of the cave and hold the lamp.

"Pass me the lamp," his uncle said, "then I will help you out."

"Help me out first, Uncle," Aladdin replied, "and then I will give you the lamp."

"No!" the man shouted. "First give me the lamp!"

When Aladdin refused, the man became angry. He rolled the stone over the opening to the cave. Aladdin was trapped in the dark.

"Uncle!" Aladdin shouted. "Let me out!"

"I'm not your uncle!" the man shouted back. "I'm a sorcerer! If you won't give me the lamp, you can stay there and die!"

Aladdin wrung his hands in despair, which rubbed the magic ring on his finger. To Aladdin's great surprise, a genie sprang out of the ring.

"What do you require, Master?" asked the genie.

Aladdin told the genie to take him home, and Aladdin found himself outside his mother's house. He told her everything that had happened, and she hugged him with relief.

Still poor and hungry, Aladdin polished the old lamp. He hoped to sell it to get money for food. But as he rubbed the lamp clean, another genie jumped out.

46

"What do you require, Lord?" asked the genie of the lamp.

Aladdin asked for food and money, so that he and his mother could live in comfort.

Life went on happily. Then one day, Aladdin fell hopelessly in love with the emperor's beautiful daughter. But how could he marry a princess?

Suddenly, Aladdin had an idea … He asked the genie for beautiful gifts to give to the princess.

When the princess thanked Aladdin for the gifts, she fell in love with him, too. Soon they were married, and Aladdin asked the genie to build them a beautiful palace.

The wicked sorcerer heard that a wealthy stranger had married the princess and guessed that Aladdin had escaped from the cave with the lamp.

So the sorcerer disguised himself as a poor tradesman. He waited for Aladdin to go out, then stood outside his palace.

"New lamps for old!" he called out.

Aladdin's wife gave her husband's old brass lamp to the sorcerer, who snatched it away. He rubbed the lamp and commanded the genie to carry the palace and the princess far away.

"Where is my beautiful wife?" cried Aladdin, when he returned.

He rubbed the magic ring to make the genie appear.

"Please bring back my wife and palace!" Aladdin pleaded.

"Sorry, Master, I can't!" said the genie of the ring. "I am less powerful than the genie of the lamp."

"Then take me to her, and I'll win her back!" Aladdin cried.

At once, Aladdin found himself in a strange city but outside his palace. Through a window he saw his wife crying.

But the sorcerer was sleeping.

Aladdin crept into the palace. He grabbed the magic lamp and rubbed it.

"What do you require, Lord?" asked the genie of the lamp.

"Take us home," Aladdin said. "And shut this wicked sorcerer in the cave for a thousand years!"

In a moment, the palace was back where it belonged.

At last, Aladdin and the princess were safe, and they never needed to call on a genie again!

I Love You, Little Bear

Little Bear and Grandma were eating breakfast.

"Grandma," asked Little Bear suddenly, "why do I have such a big nose?"

"To help you find food," Grandma told him.

"But I just looked around and I found these berries," argued Little Bear.

"Ah!" replied Grandma. "Food isn't always that easy to see."

Grandma led Little Bear down to the river.

"Can you see anything to eat?" she asked.

Little Bear shook his head.

"Can you smell anything?" Grandma added.

"Food," answered Little Bear.

"Then use your nose to find it," Grandma told him.

Little Bear followed his nose to some stones on the riverbank. He turned one over.

"A fish!" he laughed. "Yum!"

"Dinner," said Grandma. "Good work, Little Bear!"

"I love you, Grandma," Little Bear whispered in her ear.

"Grandma," asked Little Bear suddenly, "why do I have such sharp claws?"

"To help you find food," came the reply.

"But you told me I have my nose for that," said Little Bear, surprised.

"Ah!" said Grandma. "Sometimes your nose leads you to food, but you still have to work to get it."

She took Little Bear to the woods. "Sniff the air!" she said.

Little Bear followed his nose. He stopped at a fallen tree.

"I can smell food," Little Bear said. "I still can't see it, but I know it's here."

"You'll need to use your claws," Grandma told him.

Little Bear dug his sharp claws into the bark. He broke off a small piece.

"Ants!" he laughed. "Delicious!"

"Lunch," smiled Grandma. "Good work, Little Bear!

"I love you, Grandma!" Little Bear yelled.

"Grandma," asked Little Bear suddenly, "why do I have such a long tongue?"

"To help you find food," Grandma said at once.

"But you told me that I have my nose and claws to do that," said Little Bear, surprised.

"Sometimes the best food is hard to reach," Grandma told him.

She took Little Bear to a clearing.

"Smell the air," Grandma said.

Little Bear sniffed hard. He lifted his nose.

"Food!" he told Grandma. A huge bees' nest hung from a branch above him.

"I know what to do," laughed Little Bear. "Look at me!"

He hooked the nest with his sharp claws, lifted it down, and opened it up.

"Honey!" he smiled. "Mmmmm!"

"Supper," said Grandma. But Little Bear's big claws couldn't reach the food.

"So what are you going to do now?" asked Grandma.

"Use my long tongue," laughed Little Bear.

And that's just what he did.

"Brilliant, Little Bear!" laughed Grandma.

"How do you know so many things, Grandma?" asked Little Bear suddenly.

"That's easy," Grandma smiled. "When I was little, I was curious … just like you," she said.

"You ask so many questions, you'll soon know lots of things, too."

And she hugged Little Bear tight.

"Do you know I love you, Grandma?" asked Little Bear.

"I do!" answered Grandma stroking Little Bear's sticky head.

"And you know I love you, too," she said.

The Town Mouse and the Country Mouse

Once upon a time, there were two little mice. One mouse lived in the town. The other mouse lived in the country.

One day, Town Mouse went to visit Country Mouse. He had never been to the country before, so he was very excited. He packed a small suitcase and went on his way.

Country Mouse's home was small and dark— not at all like Town Mouse's home. Lunch was very different, too. There was creamy cheese, juicy apples, and crunchy hazelnuts. It was all very tasty. But Town Mouse was left feeling hungry.

After lunch, Country Mouse took Town Mouse for a walk.

They went down a path, through a gate, and into a large field. Town Mouse was just starting to enjoy himself when ...

"Moo!"

"What was that?" he asked nervously, scurrying closer to Country Mouse.

"Just a cow," said his friend. "There are lots of them in the country. It's nothing to be scared of."

Town Mouse and Country Mouse strolled on, through a meadow and over a hill. Soon they came to a pond. Town Mouse was just starting to enjoy himself when ...

"Hiss!"

"What was that?" he asked again, quivering from nose to tail.

"Just a goose," said his friend. "There are lots of them in the country. It's nothing to be scared of."

So they kept going across a bridge, down a track, and into a wood.

Town Mouse was just starting to enjoy himself when ...

"Twit-twoo!"

"What was that?" he yelped, jumping in terror.

"It's an owl!" cried Country Mouse. "Quick, run, or it will eat you!"

So the two friends ran and ran until they found a hedge to hide in.

Town Mouse was terrified.

"I don't like the country!" he said. "Come to the town and stay with me. You'll see for yourself how much better it is!"

Country Mouse had never been to the town before, so he packed a small rucksack and went to stay with his friend.

Town Mouse's home was huge and grand—not at all like Country Mouse's house.

Lunch was different, too! There were so many sandwiches and cupcakes and chocolates to eat. It was tasty, but soon Country Mouse began to feel a bit sick.

After dinner, the friends went out for a walk. They passed shops and offices and houses. Country Mouse was just starting to enjoy himself when ...

"Beep-beep!"

"What's that?" he asked fearfully, looking around.

"Just a car," said his friend. "There are lots here. It's nothing to be afraid of."

Then they walked down a wide road. Country Mouse was just starting to enjoy himself when ...

"Nee-nah! Nee-nah!"

"What's that?" he asked again, his whiskers twitching.

"Just a fire engine. There are lots of them here. It's nothing to be afraid of."

On the way home, the mice passed a playground, a school, and a pretty garden. Country Mouse was just starting to enjoy himself when ...

"Meow!"

"What's that?" he squeaked, his eyes as wide as saucers.

"It's a cat!" cried Town Mouse. "Quick, run, or it will eat you!"

So the two mice ran all the way back to Town Mouse's home.

Country Mouse was terrified! "I don't like the town! I'm going home," he said.

"But how can you be happy living near the cow and the goose and that horrible owl?" asked Town Mouse.

"They don't scare me!" cried Country Mouse. "How can you be happy living near the cars and the fire engines and that terrible cat?"

"They don't scare me!" cried Town Mouse.

The two mice looked at each other. Who was right and who was wrong? They would simply never agree. So Town Mouse went back to his grand home, and Country Mouse went back to his cozy one.

And the two of them lived happily ever after, each in their own separate way.

Thumbelina

There was once a poor woman who lived in a cottage. She had no husband, but she longed to have a child. One day, she visited a fairy to ask for her help.

"You are a good woman," said the fairy, "so I will give you this magic seed. Plant it and water it, and you will see what you will see."

The woman thanked the fairy and did as she was told. A few days later, a flower bud appeared. It had glossy pink petals wrapped tightly around its center.

"What a beautiful flower you will be," smiled the woman.

She kissed it gently, and the petals unfolded. In the center of the flower was a beautiful girl the size of a thumb. The woman was overjoyed.

"I will call you Thumbelina," she cried.

She laid her new child in a walnut-shell bed with a rose-petal quilt.

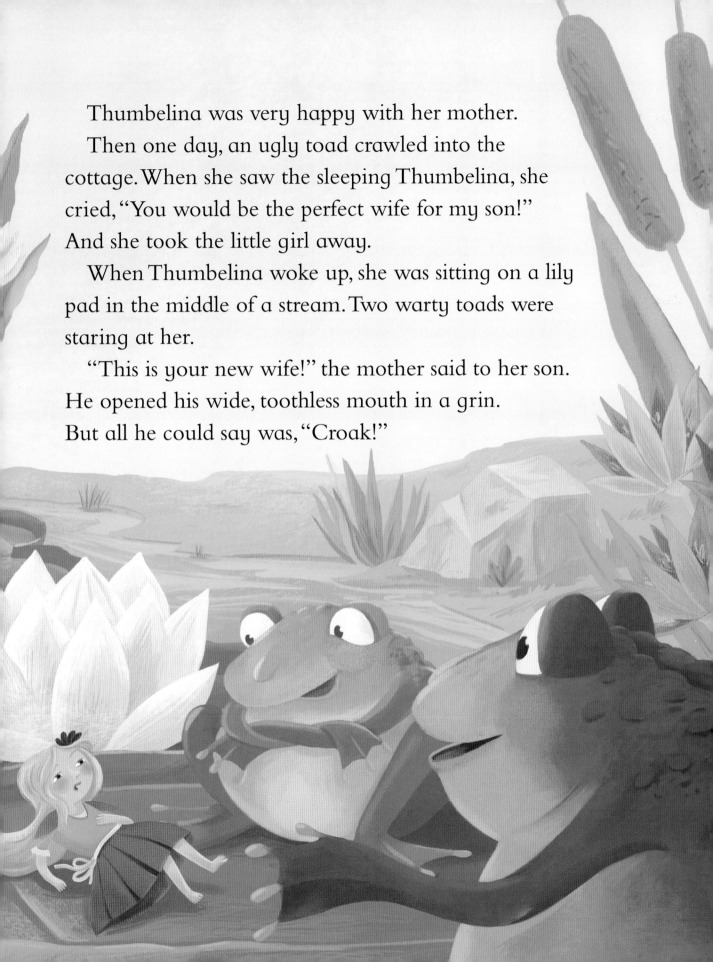

Thumbelina was very happy with her mother.

Then one day, an ugly toad crawled into the cottage. When she saw the sleeping Thumbelina, she cried, "You would be the perfect wife for my son!" And she took the little girl away.

When Thumbelina woke up, she was sitting on a lily pad in the middle of a stream. Two warty toads were staring at her.

"This is your new wife!" the mother said to her son. He opened his wide, toothless mouth in a grin. But all he could say was, "Croak!"

"I don't want to marry a toad," Thumbelina sobbed.

"You ungrateful girl!" the mother toad scolded her. "You'll stay here until you stop crying." The two toads jumped into the water and swam away.

Thumbelina sobbed and sobbed until a fish took pity on her. It nibbled through the lily pad's stem until Thumbelina floated free. She drifted downstream to the riverbank and climbed onto dry land.

Thumbelina lived there all summer long. She had no idea how to find her way home to her mother. So she busied herself collecting wild berries and making friends with the birds and small creatures.

Then winter came. Thumbelina was cold and hungry and all alone.

Luckily, a kind field mouse found her and invited her to stay with him in his burrow. Thumblina was so grateful that she agreed.

Life underground was warm and snug, but Thumbelina soon missed the sunshine. And then Mouse's friend Mole asked her to marry him.

"I don't want to marry a mole," cried Thumbelina.

"You ungrateful girl!" said the mouse. So Thumbelina agreed to marry the mole, and a date was set for the following summer.

Thumbelina was miserable.

Then one day, she walked along the underground tunnels and found a swallow. He was very cold and almost dead. She hugged the bird tightly to warm him, and he slowly opened his eyes.

"You saved my life," said the swallow. "Come with me to the South. It's the land of sunshine and flowers."

"I cannot leave Mouse," sighed Thumbelina, "he has been so kind to me."

"Then I must go alone," said the swallow. "I will return next summer. Goodbye!" Then he flew away.

Months later, the day of Thumbelina and Mole's wedding arrived. Thumbelina was so sad. As she waited for Mole to arrive, the swallow appeared again.

"Come with me now!" he cried.

This time Thumbelina said, "I will!"

So Thumbelina flew away to the South with the swallow. Once there, a beautiful flower opened in front of her. A fairy prince was in the center. He was no bigger than a thumb and had beautiful butterfly wings.

"Will you be my wife?" he asked at once.

"I will!" cried Thumbelina.

So they married, and Thumbelina became Queen of the flower fairies.

She did not forget her mother and arranged for fairy messengers to deliver a letter to her with a bouquet of flowers.

And Thumbelina and her handsome prince lived happily ever after.

The Tortoise and the Hare

The tortoise and the hare were neighbors.

Hare was always in a hurry. But Tortoise was happy just to plod steadily along.

One day, Tortoise was walking slowly along the road when Hare sped past him.

"Hurry up, Tortoise, or you'll never get there!" he shouted.

"I will," Tortoise said calmly. "Slow but steady."

Hare turned back and ran around Tortoise three times, laughing. Then he ran on.

Half an hour later, Hare came back. Tortoise was still going in the same direction. He hadn't gotten very far.

Hare laughed.

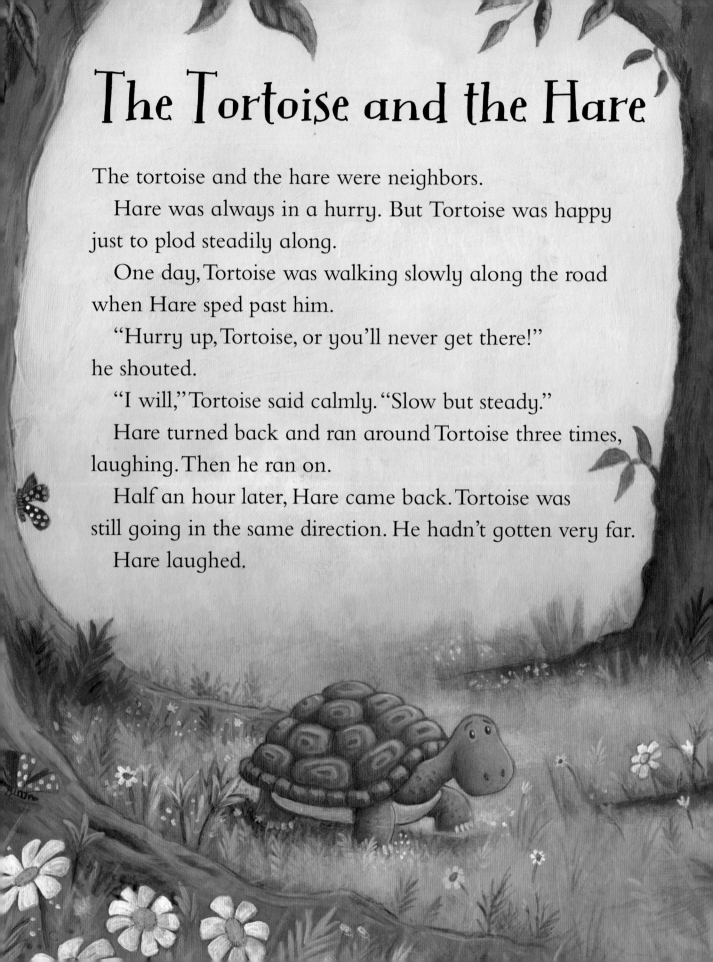

"You're so slow!" he said. "How do you get anywhere?"

"One step at a time," Tortoise said. "One foot after the other. Slow but steady."

"It will take you all day just to get to the end of the road!" laughed Hare."

Tortoise was too cross to ignore Hare any longer.

"I get everywhere I want to go!" he said. "And if you don't believe me, I'll challenge you to a race."

Hare laughed until he fell over. He rolled around on the floor, tears running along his whiskers.

"A race?" he gasped. "Between you and me? You don't stand a chance."

"Are you scared?" Tortoise asked. "Because if not, let's do it."

So they planned the race for the next day and asked Fox to judge it. They would start from an old oak tree and race all the way to the river.

Tortoise set out early that evening, so that he would be at the start line on time in the morning.

Hare went home for a long sleep and got up late. He ran to the oak tree and found Tortoise ready and waiting. All the other animals had come out to watch.

"Fox is waiting for you at the river," Bear said. "We can start whenever you're ready."

So the tortoise and the hare got into position and off they went.

Tortoise lifted one foot and put it down. Then he lifted the other foot and put it down. Slow but steady.

But Hare sprinted off ahead.

After a few minutes, Hare could see the river. He paused and looked around. He couldn't see Tortoise at all.

"He is so slow!" he laughed to himself. "He won't be here for hours. I might as well take a rest." Hare sat down under a tree not far from the finish line. Soon Hare dozed off.

Back along the path, Tortoise continued. Slow but steady. One step at a time. One foot after the other.

To the river

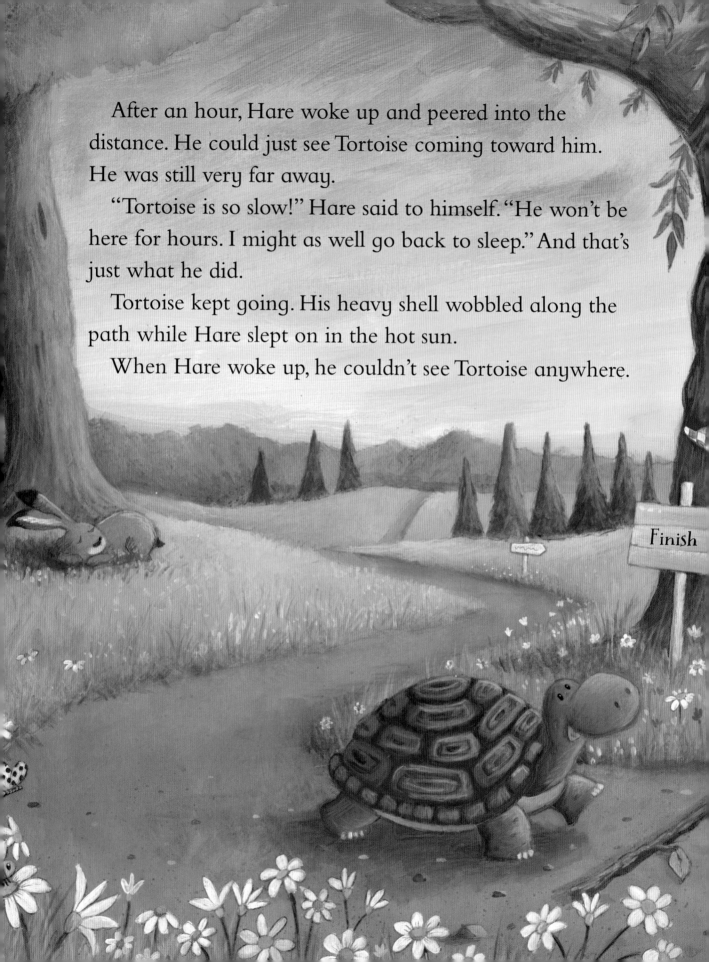

After an hour, Hare woke up and peered into the distance. He could just see Tortoise coming toward him. He was still very far away.

"Tortoise is so slow!" Hare said to himself. "He won't be here for hours. I might as well go back to sleep." And that's just what he did.

Tortoise kept going. His heavy shell wobbled along the path while Hare slept on in the hot sun.

When Hare woke up, he couldn't see Tortoise anywhere.

Finish

"Where is he?" he said. "He won't be here for hours. I could just go back to sleep."

But the sun was setting low in the sky.

"I'm sick of this race," he thought. "I should finish so I can go home and nap in my own bed." And he sprang up and ran as fast as he could to the finish line.

Tortoise was waiting for him by the river.

"Where have you been?" asked Tortoise. "I've been here for hours. You are so slow!"

Hare tried to explain, but neither Tortoise nor Fox would listen.

"But I'm faster!" Hare complained. "It's not fair!"

"The rules were simple," Fox said. "Tortoise won."

"The race was to get here first," Tortoise smiled, "not to run fastest. Slow and steady wins the race!"

The Snow Queen

Once upon a time, there was a wicked elf. He made a magic mirror that showed everything in a bad light. The mirror broke into hundreds of pieces, and shards of glass flew out around the world.

Meanwhile, a little boy named Kai and a little girl named Gerda grew up with each other. They were like brother and sister.

One day, a shard of the broken mirror went in Kai's eye. Kai became very cold and unfriendly. Poor Gerda had no idea what had happened to her friend.

"Come and play with me, Kai," she begged.

"I don't want to play with you anymore. Leave me alone," said Kai.

Kai liked the cold and the ice. Snowflakes became his favorite thing. He spent all day looking at snowflakes and the pretty shapes they made.

Before long, the Snow Queen herself noticed Kai.

74

One day, she came to see him.

"I can take you to a place where it is always cold and snowy," she said. So Kai went away with her.

Nobody knew where Kai had gone. Some thought he was dead. But Gerda felt in her heart that Kai was still alive. So she set off to find him, wearing a pair of new red shoes.

After awhile, Gerda came to a river.

"River, have you seen my friend Kai?" she asked. But the river did not reply.

"I will give you my new shoes if you will help me," she told the river. And she threw her shoes into the water.

The river replied:

"In my murky waters deep, many secrets do I keep. But no boy rested his head upon my muddy riverbed."

Gerda was relieved that Kai had not drowned. So she set off again. She walked for many miles until she came to a beautiful garden where she stopped to rest. She lay down and fell asleep.

When she woke up, a beautiful rose spoke to her:

"Beneath the ground where roots run deep, I cannot see your friend asleep."

Gerda was happy because this meant that Kai wasn't dead. So she set off once more to look for her dear friend.

While Gerda was walking through a forest, she met a reindeer.

"Reindeer, have you seen my friend Kai?" she asked him.

"Is he the boy who likes snowflakes?" replied the reindeer.

"Yes, they are his favorite thing," said Gerda.

The kind reindeer told Gerda that he had seen Kai in the grounds of the Snow Queen's palace.

"Climb onto my back and I'll take you there," he said.

Gerda was so happy. She would soon find Kai and take him home. But the Snow Queen's land was guarded by snowflakes.

"How will we ever get past these snowflakes?" thought Gerda. But as she walked through them, they were melted by the warmth of her heart.

Gerda and the reindeer searched everywhere for Kai in the icy land. Suddenly, Gerda saw her old friend sitting in the middle of a frozen lake.

"There he is!" she gasped. She rushed over.

"Who are you?" said Kai coldly. "Leave me alone."

But Gerda flung her arms around him and would not let go. She cried so hard that Kai's icy heart began to melt.

Soon Kai started crying as well. His own tears washed the shard of broken mirror from his eye.

"Gerda, is it really you?" asked Kai.

"Yes, I've come to take you home," she replied. But Kai noticed the Snow Queen riding toward them.

"We must leave this place quickly," warned Kai. "Or the Snow Queen will freeze our hearts and make us stay here."

So Kai and Gerda climbed onto the reindeer's back and rode away from the icy land.

They never saw the Snow Queen again and they lived happily ever after.

Puss in Boots

There was once an old miller who had three sons.

The miller died and left the mill to his oldest son.

The middle son was given the donkeys.

The youngest son was a kind man who had always put his father and brothers before himself. But his father only left him his cat.

"What will become of me?" sighed the young miller's son, looking at his father's cat.

"Buy me a fine pair of boots, and I will help you make your fortune," replied the cat. "Your father thought you deserved it."

A talking cat! The miller's son could not believe it.

So he bought the cat a fine pair of boots, and the two of them set off to seek their fortune.

After awhile, they came to a grand palace.

"Wouldn't it be wonderful to live so grandly," said the miller's son.

Later, the cat went hunting and caught a rabbit. He put it in a sack and took it to the palace.

"A gift to the king from my master, the Marquis of Carabas," said the cat. He was pretending the miller's son was a grand nobleman.

The cat went back to the miller's son and told him what he had done.

"Now the king will want to know all about you," laughed the cat.

The cat delivered gifts all that week, and the king became very curious. He decided his daughter should meet this mysterious Marquis of Carabas.

When the cat heard that the king and his daughter were on their way, he wasted no time.

"You must take off all your clothes and stand in the river," the cat told his master.

The puzzled miller's son did as he was told, and the cat hid his master's tattered old clothes behind a rock.

The cat heard the king's carriage approaching. So he jumped onto the road and begged for help.

"Your gracious majesty," said the cat, "my master was robbed of all his clothes while he was bathing in the river."

The king gave the miller's son a suit of fine clothes to wear.

"Please join us in the carriage," said the king.

So the cat opened the door and the miller's son climbed in. He looked very handsome in his new suit. The king's daughter fell in love with him at once.

The cat ran on through the surrounding countryside.

He told everyone he saw, "Tell the king this land belongs to the Marquis of Carabas."

It wasn't long before the cat reached a grand castle. He spoke to the people working in a field next to it and discovered that it belonged to a fierce ogre. The cat stood bravely in his boots and knocked on the castle door.

"I have heard that you are a clever ogre," the cat called out. "I would like to see what tricks you can do."

The ogre liked to show off and opened the door. He quickly changed himself into a snarling lion.

"Very clever," said the cat. "But a lion is large, and I think it would be more impressive to change into a small mouse."

At once, the ogre changed into a little mouse. The cat pounced on him and ate him up!

Then the cat went into the castle and told all of the servants that their new master was the Marquis of Carabas. They were glad the ogre was gone, so they did not complain.

"The king is on his way to visit," said the cat. "Prepare a grand feast to welcome him."

The cat was waiting at the castle when the king's royal carriage arrived.

"Welcome to the home of my master, the Marquis of Carabas," purred the cat.

A cunning cat! The miller's son could not believe it.

"You must ask for the princess's hand in marriage," whispered the cat to his master. So he did!

The king was impressed by everything he saw and agreed.

Soon the Marquis of Carabas and the princess were married. The cat was made a lord of their court and given the most splendid clothes to wear with his fine boots.

And they all lived happily ever after.

The Lion and the Mouse

Once there was a huge lion who lived in a dark den.

The lion loved to sleep in his den when he wasn't hunting. If the lion didn't get enough sleep, he became extremely grumpy.

One day, a little mouse took a shortcut home straight through the lion's den.

"What harm can it do?" he thought. "The lion is snoring too loudly to hear me."

He hurried past the sleeping beast and accidentally ran over the lion's paw. The lion woke up and gave a mighty roar. Then he grabbed the little mouse in one quick motion.

"How dare you wake me up!" the lion roared angrily. "Don't you know who I am? I am King of the Beasts! No one disturbs my sleep. I will kill you and eat you for my supper." He opened his huge mouth wide.

The terrified little mouse shook with fear at the sight of all the lion's sharp teeth. He begged the angry lion to let him go.

"Please, Your Majesty," he cried. "I didn't mean to wake you up. It was an accident. I was just trying to get home. I'm too small to make a good meal for someone as mighty as you. Let me go, and I promise to help you one day."

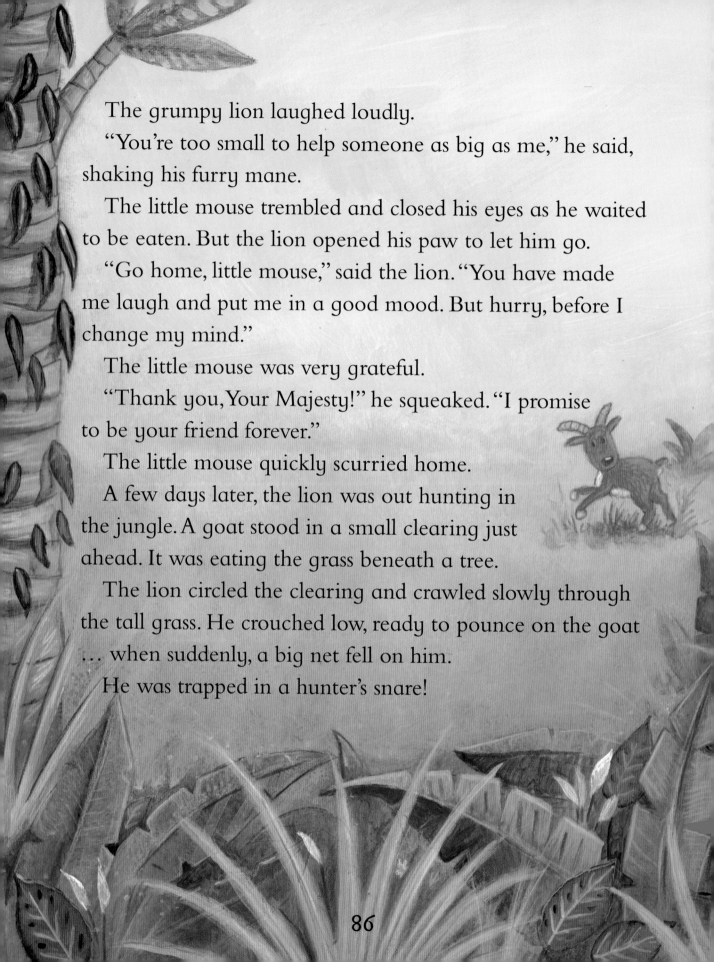

The grumpy lion laughed loudly.

"You're too small to help someone as big as me," he said, shaking his furry mane.

The little mouse trembled and closed his eyes as he waited to be eaten. But the lion opened his paw to let him go.

"Go home, little mouse," said the lion. "You have made me laugh and put me in a good mood. But hurry, before I change my mind."

The little mouse was very grateful.

"Thank you, Your Majesty!" he squeaked. "I promise to be your friend forever."

The little mouse quickly scurried home.

A few days later, the lion was out hunting in the jungle. A goat stood in a small clearing just ahead. It was eating the grass beneath a tree.

The lion circled the clearing and crawled slowly through the tall grass. He crouched low, ready to pounce on the goat … when suddenly, a big net fell on him.

He was trapped in a hunter's snare!

The goat bleated in terror and ran off into the jungle. The lion roared and tried to break free from the trap. But the more he struggled, the more he became tangled in the net. He was so angry that he let out the loudest of roars.

The trees in the jungle shook with the terrible noise. Every animal for miles heard it ... including the little mouse.

RROOAARR!

"Oh no!" squeaked the mouse. "That's my lion friend. He must be in trouble! I've got to go and help him."

The little mouse scurried through the jungle toward the lion's mighty roar.

Soon he came upon the clearing. He saw the lion. He was tangled and trapped in the ropes of the hunter's net.

"Keep still, Your Majesty," cried the mouse. "I'll have you out of there in no time."

"You?" laughed the lion.

The mouse ignored him and started gnawing through the net with his sharp little teeth.

Before long, there was a big hole in the net. The lion squeezed through the ropes and escaped his trap.

The lion held out his giant paw toward the little mouse.

"Thank you," he said humbly. "I was wrong to laugh at you. You saved my life today. I am truly grateful."

The little mouse smiled up at the lion. "You were kind enough to let me go before," he squeaked. "It was my turn to help you."

And the huge, mighty lion and the tiny, mighty mouse became the best of friends.

A Sailor Went to Sea

A sailor went to sea, sea, sea.
To see what he could see, see, see.
But all that he could see, see, see,
Was the bottom of the deep blue
sea, sea, sea.

Long-Legged Sailor

Have you ever, ever, ever,
in your long-legged life
met a long-legged sailor
with a long-legged wife?

No, I never, never, never,
in my long-legged life
met a long-legged sailor
with a long-legged wife.

*(Repeat the rhyme four more times,
using the different words.)*

Have you ever, ever, ever,
in your short-legged life ...

Have you ever, ever, ever,
in your knock-kneed life ...

Have you ever, ever, ever,
in your pigeon-toed life ...

Have you ever, ever, ever,
in your bow-legged life ...

Lavender's Blue

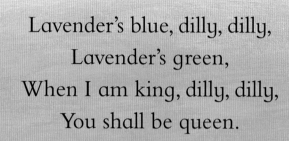

Lavender's blue, dilly, dilly,
Lavender's green,
When I am king, dilly, dilly,
You shall be queen.

Call up your men, dilly, dilly,
Set them to work,
Some with a rake, dilly, dilly,
Some with a fork.

Some to make hay, dilly, dilly,
Some to thresh corn,
While you and I, dilly, dilly,
Keep ourselves warm.